T0034008

Howard Kasschau Piano Course

TEACH ME TO PLAY

REVISED EDITION

PRIVATE or CLASS
INSTRUCTION

*A Preliminary Book
for the
Earliest Beginner*

Illustrated by Josine Ianco Kline

ED. 2336

G. SCHIRMER, Inc.

DISTRIBUTED BY

HAL•LEONARD°
CORPORATION
7777 W. BLUEMOUND RD. P.O. BOX 13819 MILWAUKEE, WI 53213

TO THE TEACHER

You, the teacher, are the inspiration that leads the young piano student step by step and lesson by lesson through the exciting experience of piano study. It is the aim of **Teach Me To Play** to assist you in imparting your musical knowledge to your pupil in a constantly interesting, logical and progressive manner, so that he may one day share your enthusiasm for the art of music. This book has been graded very gradually in order to guide the pupil's progress at the piano a step at a time. It is also an activity book to be read *by* the teacher *with* the pupil. In this way each new musical experience is approached by the pupil in four ways:

1 by explanation,

2 by actual writing,

3 by reading music,

4 by playing.

How To Use This Book

Teach Me To Play is an introductory book to piano study for the young beginner. It is designed to cover approximately the first half of the first season's lessons. While the lessons have not been separately numbered (Lesson One, Lesson Two, etc.), each lesson consists of explanatory and written material including a piece which is based upon the new musical experience. With some pupils, however, it will be found possible to cover several pieces together with their explanatory and written material in a single lesson. You, the teacher, are in the best position to determine how much material may be given to a student during a single lesson because you are most aware of his or her musical aptitude.

Teach Me To Play starts with the Middle C approach. It begins with three notes in each hand (C D E in the right hand and A B C in the left hand), expanding one note at a time until all the fingers of both hands are in this position:

Following this, *Teach Me To Play* introduces and develops three fundamental positions together with their key signatures. Material is then provided for the pupil to play in these three positions:

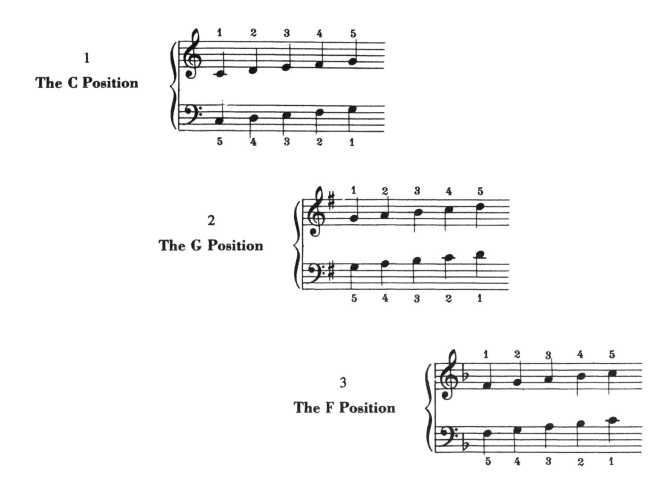

1
The C Position

2
The G Position

3
The F Position

The establishment of these three positions enables the young student to enjoy the variety that occurs when playing in key centers other than the key of C. This stimulates his musical interest. The technical problems of playing in the C F and G positions are solved in a simple manner in *Teach Me To Play*. Therefore, the young pianist is able to make use of the large amount of very easy supplementary material that is so very necessary for his musical progress.

May this book help you in your teaching as it has helped me in mine!

Howard Kasschau

CONTENTS

Finding Middle C

Let us look at the KEYBOARD. There are **WHITE** keys and **BLACK** keys.

The **BLACK** keys are in groups. Some groups have **TWO** BLACK keys and some groups have **THREE** BLACK keys.

Here is a picture of the KEYBOARD. Above each group of **TWO** BLACK keys mark the number **2**, and above each group of **THREE** BLACK keys mark the number **3**:

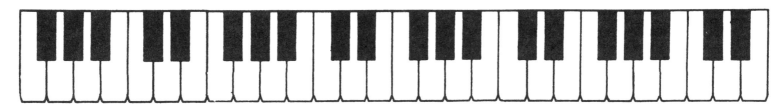

Look at the **TWO** BLACK KEYS. The **WHITE** key just to the LEFT of each group of **TWO** BLACK keys is **C**. There are several **C**'s on the KEYBOARD.

Here is another keyboard picture. Mark the letter **C** on each key named **C**:

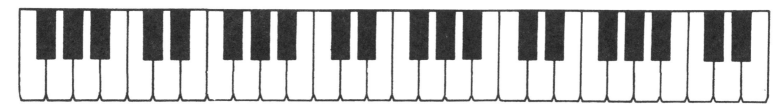

With one finger let us play every **C**.

Just to the RIGHT of C is **D**. Find some more **D**'s on the KEYBOARD.

Just to the RIGHT of D is **E**. Find some more **E**'s on the KEYBOARD.

Now we have three keys in a row: **C D E**.

On the following keyboard picture mark the letters **C D E** on each key named **C D E**:

With one finger let us play every **C D E** on the KEYBOARD.

The **C** nearest to the MIDDLE of the keyboard is called **MIDDLE C**.

Notes

This is a **NOTE:** ●

Trace around the dotted lines and then fill in the following six notes:

Sometimes the *Stems* of a note go **UP.** ♩

On the following six notes trace around the dotted lines, fill in the notes and then add stems going **UP:**

Sometimes the *Stems* of a note go **DOWN.** ♩

On the following six notes trace around the dotted lines, fill in the notes and then add stems going **DOWN:**

The notes you have written are called **QUARTER-NOTES.** Each **QUARTER-NOTE** receives **ONE COUNT.**

These are **HALF-NOTES:** ♩ ♩ . They look like quarter-notes except that they are hollow.

On the following six HALF-NOTES trace around the dotted lines and then add stems going **UP:**

On the following six HALF-NOTES trace around the dotted lines and then add stems going **DOWN:**

Each **HALF-NOTE** receives **TWO COUNTS.**

The G Clef *(TREBLE CLEF)*

This is a **G CLEF**: 𝄞

In three steps you can make a **G CLEF**.

STEP ONE

Trace the following dotted lines beginning above Line 5 for Step One:

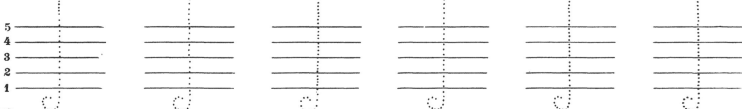

STEP TWO

Trace the following dotted lines of Steps One and Two:

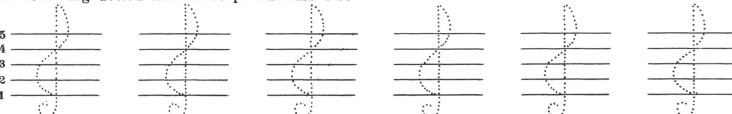

STEP THREE

Trace the following dotted lines of Steps One, Two and Three:

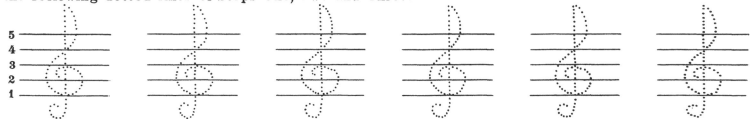

Now draw six **G CLEFS** on the following STAFFS:

1   2   3   4   5   6

The notes on the G CLEF are played by the RIGHT HAND.

C D E - Having Fun

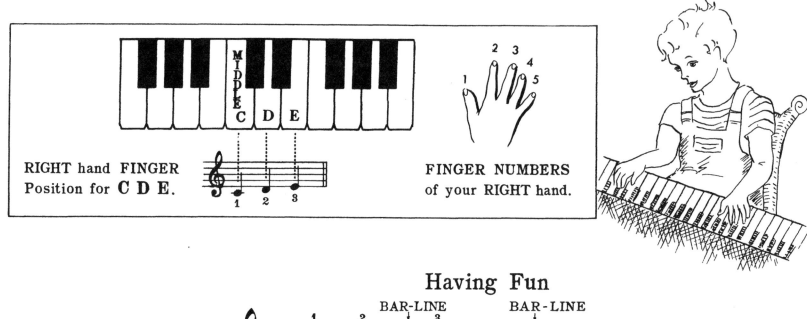

RIGHT hand **FINGER** Position for **C D E.**

FINGER NUMBERS of your **RIGHT** hand.

Having Fun

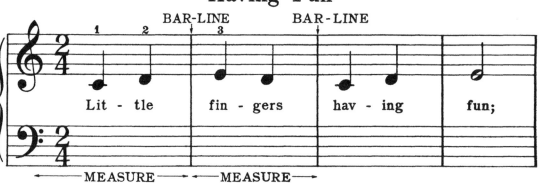

BAR-LINES divide music into MEASURES.

MEASURES divide music into groups of equal counts.

How many MEASURES are there in "Having Fun"?

Lit - tle   fin - gers   hav - ing   fun;

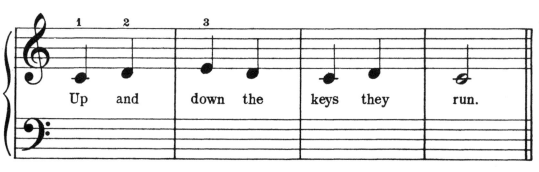

Up   and   down   the   keys   they   run.

DOUBLE BAR-LINES are always used at the end of a piece of music.

Finding A B C

Now let us look at the group of **THREE BLACK** keys.

Just to the LEFT of the third black key is **A**.

On the following keyboard picture mark the letter **A** on each key named **A**:

With one finger let us play every **A** on the keyboard.

Just to the RIGHT of **A** is **B**.

On the following keyboard picture mark the letter **B** on each key named **B**:

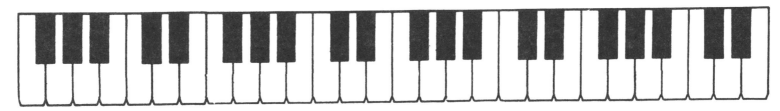

With one finger let us play every **B** on the keyboard.

Just to the RIGHT of **B** is the first note we learned, **C**.

Now we have three more notes in a row, **A B C**.

On the following keyboard picture mark the letters **A B C** on each key named **A B C**:

With one finger let us play every A B C on the keyboard.

The F Clef (BASS CLEF)

This is an F CLEF: 𝄢

In two steps you can make an **F CLEF**.

STEP ONE

Trace the following dotted lines:

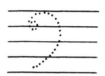 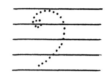 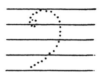 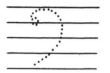 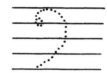

STEP TWO

Fill in the following dots on both sides of Line 4:

Now put the first and second steps together:

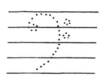 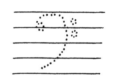 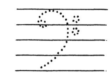

Now draw six **F CLEFS** on the following STAFFS:

| 1 | 2 | 3 | 4 | 5 | 6 |

The notes on the F CLEF are played by the **LEFT** HAND.

44543

A B C - More Fun

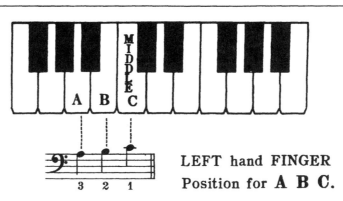

FINGER NUMBERS
of your LEFT hand.

LEFT hand FINGER
Position for **A B C.**

3 2 1

More Fun

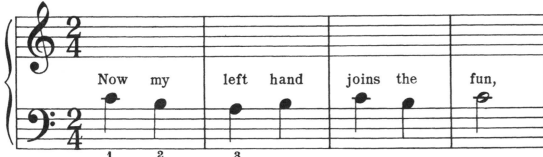

Now my | left hand | joins the | fun,

1 2 3

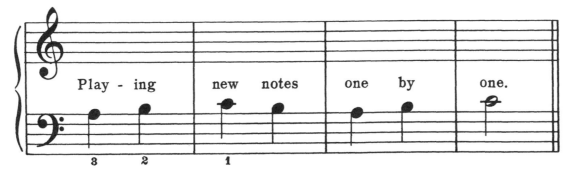

Play - ing | new notes | one by | one.

3 2 1

The Right Hand and Left Hand Middle C

This is a **RIGHT** hand MIDDLE C. The *Stem* goes **UP**.

The **RIGHT** hand MIDDLE C is on an added line *below* the G CLEF.

This is a **LEFT** hand MIDDLE C. The *Stem* goes **DOWN**.

The **LEFT** hand MIDDLE C is on an added line *above* the F CLEF.

Trace the following **RIGHT** hand MIDDLE C's:

Trace the following **LEFT** hand MIDDLE C's:

If you trace the following notes you will find that some are **RIGHT** hand MIDDLE C's and some are **LEFT** hand MIDDLE C's. On the dotted lines below each note mark **R** for **RIGHT** hand and **L** for **LEFT** hand:

Weather

Walk - ing in the rain is fun And

so is play - ing in the sun.

A New Note For Each Hand

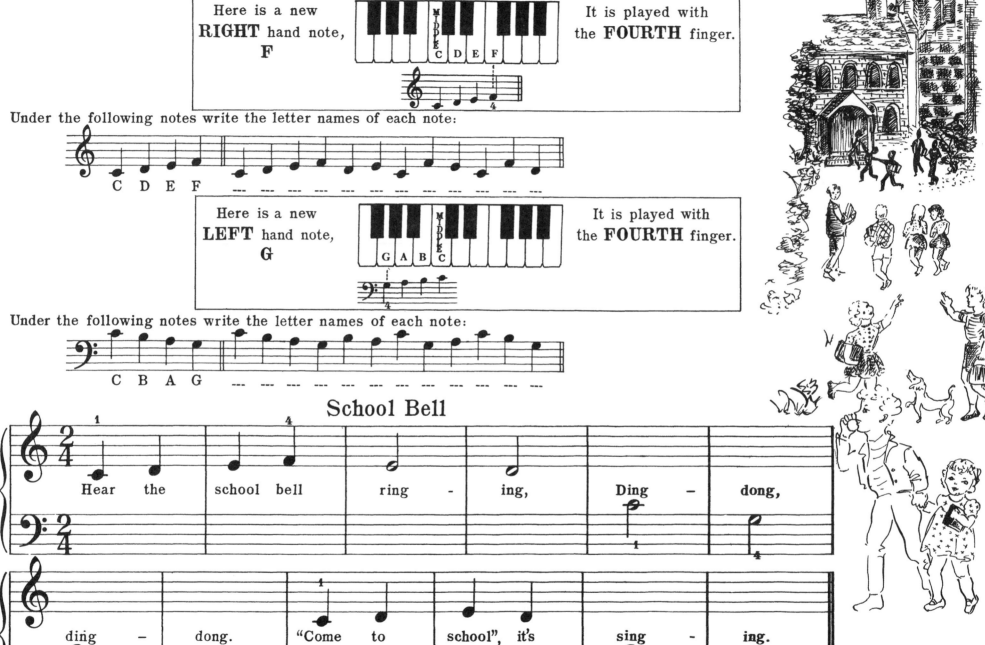

Here is a new **RIGHT** hand note, **F**

It is played with the **FOURTH** finger.

Under the following notes write the letter names of each note:

C D E F

Here is a new **LEFT** hand note, **G**

It is played with the **FOURTH** finger.

Under the following notes write the letter names of each note:

C B A G

School Bell

Hear the school bell ring - ing, Ding - dong,

ding - dong. "Come to school", it's sing - ing.

The first *seven* letters of the alphabet have been used to *name* our keys: **A B C D E F G**. These letters are the only ones used to name the keys of the entire keyboard.

On the following keyboard picture start with A and write in the letter names of all the keys:

With one finger play any C D E F and G. After G, our next note is A followed by B. Then we are ready for the next group of C D E F G.

Yankee Doodle

American Folk Song

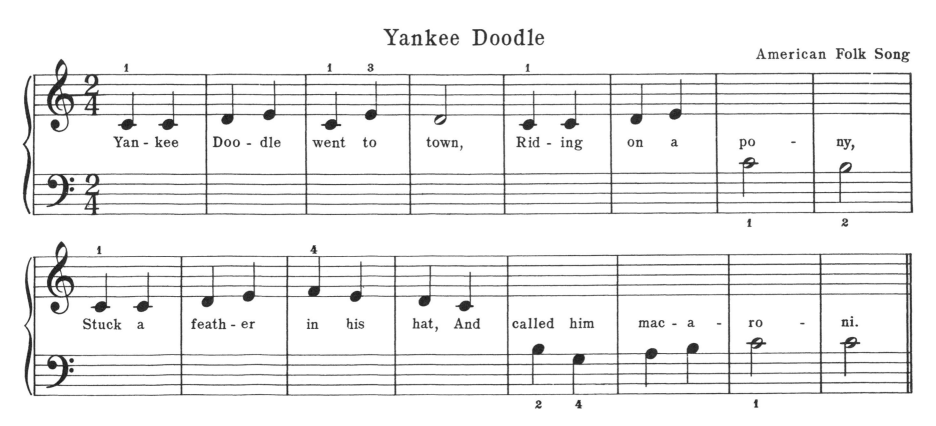

The Dotted Half-Note

This is a **DOTTED HALF-NOTE**: 𝅗𝅥. It receives **THREE** COUNTS.
It is made by placing a **DOT** after a HALF-NOTE.

Trace around the following HALF-NOTES and fill in each dot. You will make eight **DOTTED HALF-NOTES**.

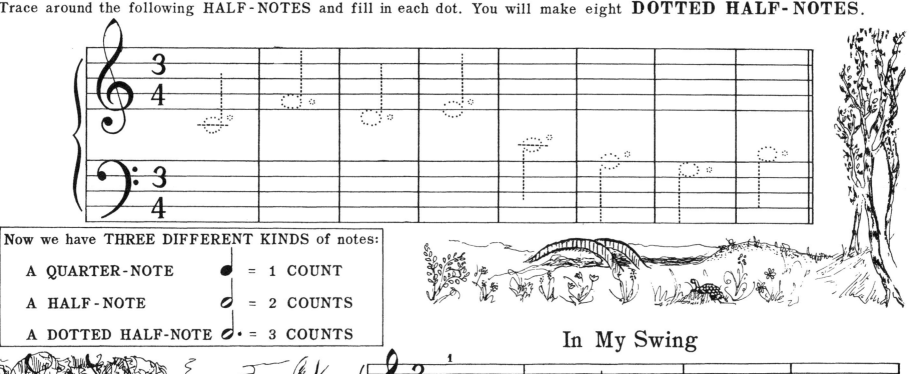

Now we have THREE DIFFERENT KINDS of notes:

A QUARTER-NOTE ♩ = 1 COUNT

A HALF-NOTE ♩ = 2 COUNTS

A DOTTED HALF-NOTE 𝅗𝅥• = 3 COUNTS

In My Swing

High, high in the sky I'm

fly - ing, fly - ing.

Time Signatures

This is a **TIME SIGNATURE**: There are **TWO** COUNTS in each measure. A **QUARTER-NOTE** receives **ONE** COUNT.

At the beginning of every piece of music there are two numbers called a **TIME SIGNATURE**. The **UPPER** NUMBER tells you HOW MANY COUNTS there are in each measure. The **LOWER** NUMBER tells you WHAT KIND of note receives **ONE** COUNT.

In the following **TIME SIGNATURES** fill in the blank spaces: _____

There are _____ COUNTS in each measure.
A _____ NOTE receives ONE COUNT.

There are _____ COUNTS in each measure.
A _____ NOTE receives ONE COUNT.

There are _____ COUNTS in each measure.
A _____ NOTE receives ONE COUNT.

Bouncing A Ball

I'm much too bus - y for talk - ing,

Bounc - ing a ball while I'm walk - ing, walk - ing.

44543   *Can you find this new note? It is explained on page **20**.

The Phrase

What is a **PHRASE?** It is a group of **MEASURES** that express a complete musical thought.

Trace the dotted line over the words of the following **PHRASE**. You will find that the FIRST PHRASE asks a question.

"Tap, tap, tap, tap. May I come in?"

Trace the dotted line over the words of the following **PHRASE**. You will find that the SECOND PHRASE answers the first phrase.

"Tell me who's there and then you may come in."

You have drawn phrase lines over two complete sentences, each expressing a complete thought.

Now play "Tap! Tap!" Notice how each phrase expresses a complete *musical* thought.

Tap! Tap!

THREE Counts in each measure.

A Quarter-Note receives ONE Count.

"Tap, tap, tap, tap. May I come in?"

"Tell me who's there and then you may come in."

The Whole Note

This is a **WHOLE NOTE:** **O**
It receives **FOUR** COUNTS.

Trace around the following WHOLE NOTES and you will make eight **WHOLE NOTES**.

Now we have FOUR DIFFERENT KINDS of notes:

A QUARTER-NOTE ♩ = 1 COUNT

A HALF-NOTE ♩ = 2 COUNTS

A DOTTED HALF-NOTE ♩. = 3 COUNTS

A WHOLE NOTE **O** = 4 COUNTS

Old MacDonald Had A Farm
American Folk Song

FOUR Counts in each measure.

A Quarter-Note receives ONE Count.

Old Mac-Don-ald had a farm. E I E I O!

On that farm he had some chicks. E I E I O!

44543

A New Note For The Right Hand

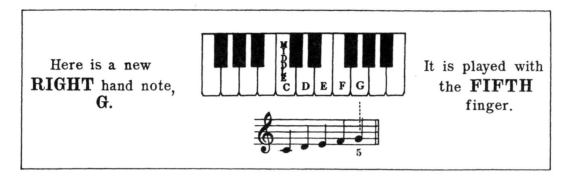

Here is a new **RIGHT** hand note, **G.**

It is played with the **FIFTH** finger.

Under the following notes write the letter name of each note:

C D E F G

Parade

Boom, boom, boom, boom! | Hear the beat-ing | of the | drum.

Tramp, tramp, tramp, tramp! | See the sol-diers | as they | come.

A New Note For The Left Hand

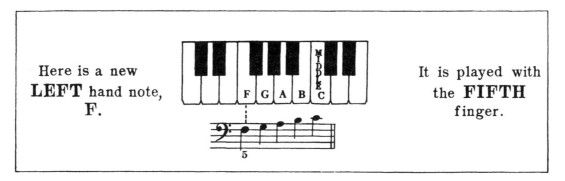

Here is a new **LEFT** hand note, **F**.

It is played with the **FIFTH** finger.

Under the following notes write the letter name of each note:

C B A G F   ___ ___ ___ ___ ___ ___ ___ ___ ___ ___ ___ ___ ___

Little Engine

I'm a lit - tle en - gine chug-ging up a hill.

"Toot! Toot!" goes my whis - tle, loud and clear and shrill. Toot! Toot!

To the Teacher: Playing hands together is explained on page 23.

The Half-Note in $\frac{3}{4}$ Time

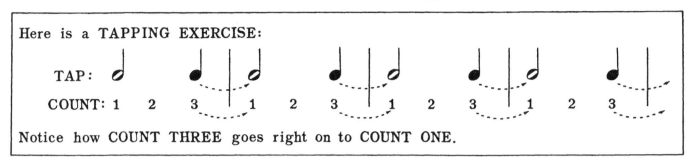

In this piece there are **THREE COUNTS** in each measure. The FIRST note in each measure receives TWO COUNTS and the SECOND note receives the THIRD COUNT.

When you play "Roly-Poly" be careful NOT to play the third count of any measure until you are ready to go right on to the first count of the next measure.

Roly-Poly

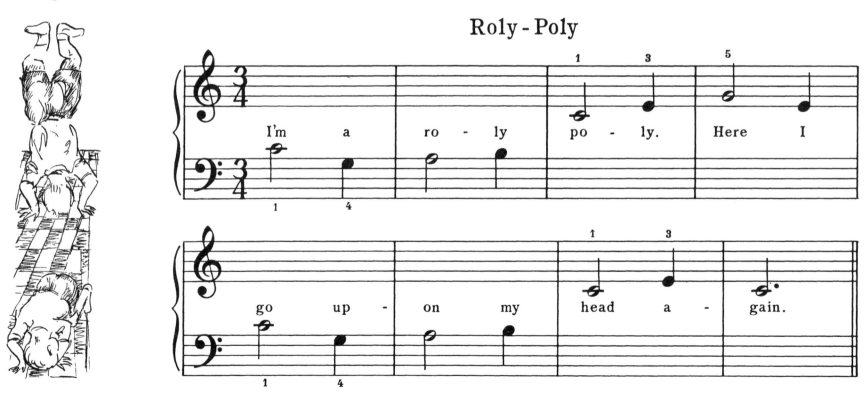

Playing Hands Together

So far, either the right hand or the left hand has played by itself. Now, for the first time, **BOTH HANDS** are going to **PLAY TOGETHER**.

When BOTH HANDS play at the *same time* the notes are placed one above the other, like this:

In the following measures some notes are played by the **RIGHT** hand, some by the **LEFT** hand and some are played by **BOTH** hands **TOGETHER**.

Under each measure: Mark **R** for the **RIGHT** hand.

L for the **LEFT** hand.

T for hands **TOGETHER**.

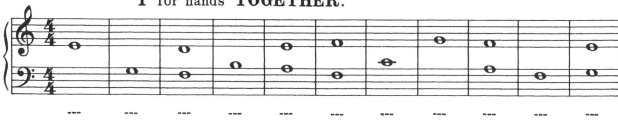

Elevator Man

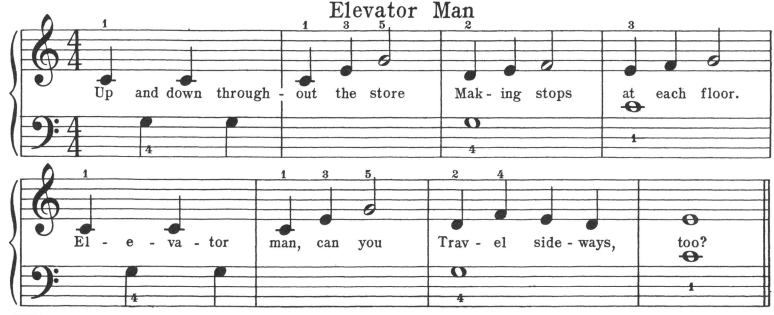

Up and down through - out the store   Mak - ing stops   at each floor.

El - e - va - tor   man, can you   Trav - el side - ways,   too?

The C Position

Here is a new position for the **LEFT** hand.

Now we have { The **RIGHT** hand **THUMB** on **MIDDLE C**.
The **LEFT** hand **FIFTH FINGER** on the first **C** *below* **MIDDLE C**.

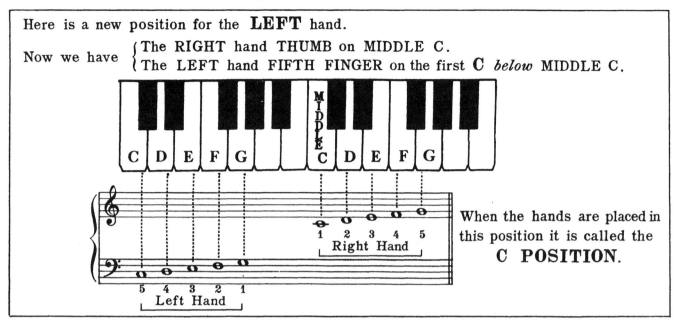

When the hands are placed in this position it is called the **C POSITION**.

Merrily We Roll Along

American Folk Song

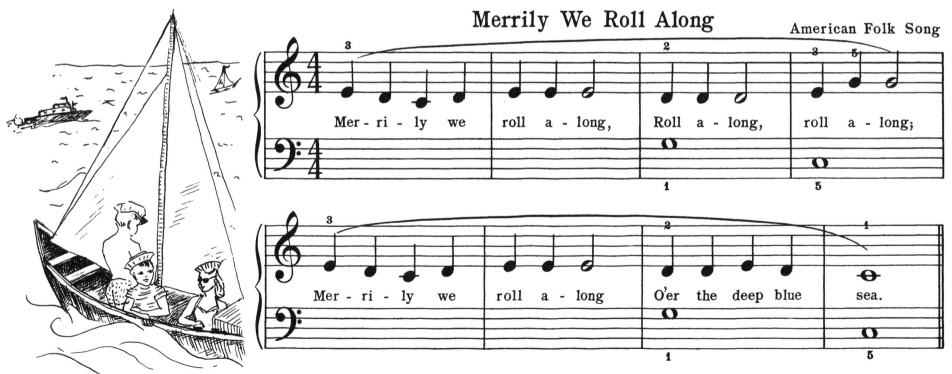

In the C POSITION the **LEFT** hand notes look like this:

Write the letter names under the following left hand notes:

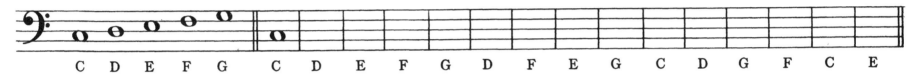

Now write whole notes over their letter names:

C D E F G C D E F G D F E G C D G F C E

Balloons

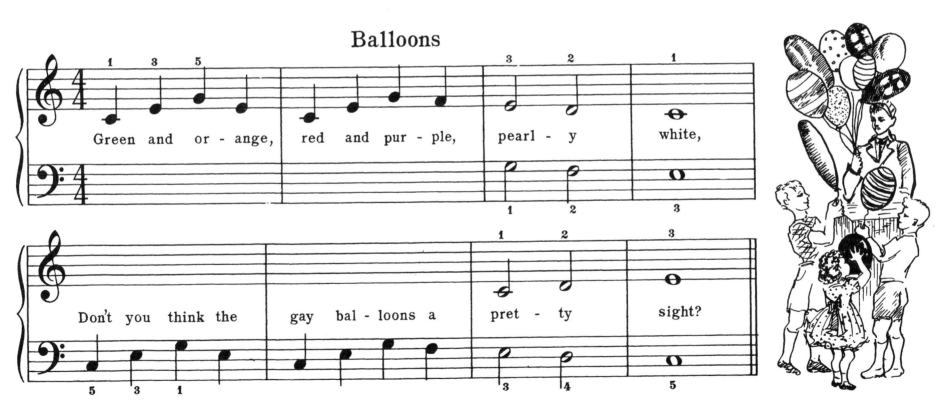

Green and or - ange, red and pur - ple, pearl - y white,

Don't you think the gay bal - loons a pret - ty sight?

The Whole Rest

This is a **WHOLE REST**:

It is a sign that is used to tell you a hand is to be *silent* for a whole measure.

Trace the following dotted lines, fill in the blank spaces and you will make six **WHOLE RESTS**.

Notice that they *hang* from the *fourth* line.

Now draw six **WHOLE RESTS**:

Dinosaur

Di - no - saur, Di - no - saur, You are so tall.

If you should stum - ble, Oh, my, what a fall!

*NOTE TO THE TEACHER: In order to accentuate "fall" you may prefer to have the student place the thumb on both C and B.

44543

Eighth-Notes

These are *single* EIGHTH-NOTES:

These are *groups* of EIGHTH-NOTES:

Trace and fill in the following notes. You will make both *single* EIGHTH-NOTES and *groups* of EIGHTH-NOTES.

Two **EIGHTH-NOTES** are played in ONE COUNT.

Here is a tapping exercise:

TAP:

COUNT: 1　　2　　1　　2　　1 - 2 -　　1 - 2 -

TWO Counts in each measure. A Quarter-Note receives ONE Count.

Trolley Ride

Clang-clang,　clang-clang,　rid-ing　on　a　trol - ley;

Must　I　pay　a　nick - el　for　my　dol - ly?

44543

Come and Dance with Me

Come and dance with me. One,— two,— three, See how we glide.

Step-ping to the right, Step-ping to the left, Back to the side.

The Half-Rest

This is a **HALF-REST**:

It is a sign that is used to tell you a hand is to be *silent* for TWO COUNTS.

Trace the following dotted lines, fill in the blank spaces and you will make six **HALF-RESTS**:

Notice that they *sit* on the *third* line.

Now draw six **HALF-RESTS**:

1   2   3   4   5   6

Hide and Seek

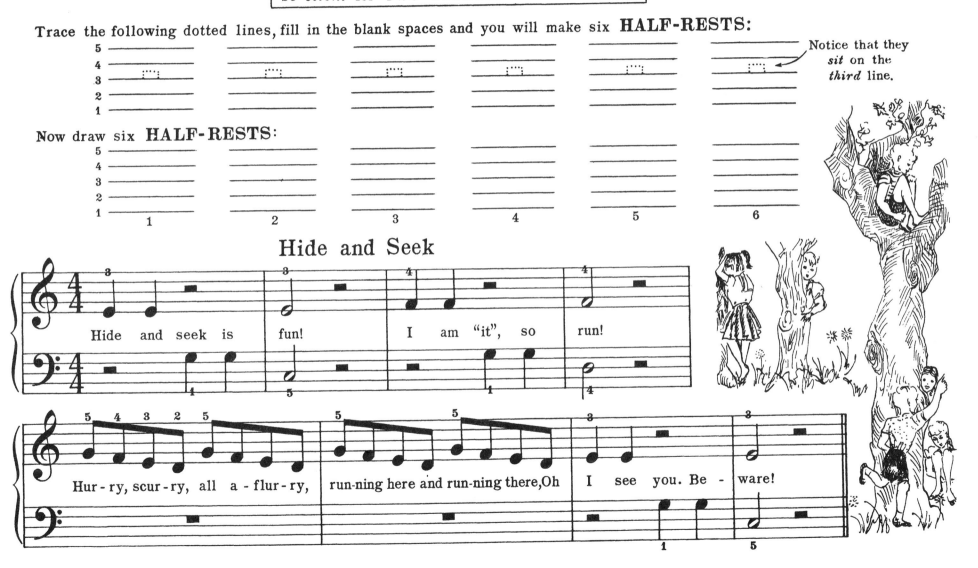

Hide and seek is fun! I am "it", so run!

Hur-ry, scur-ry, all a-flur-ry, run-ning here and run-ning there, Oh I see you. Be - ware!

The Quarter-Rest

This is a **QUARTER-REST**:

It is a sign that is used to tell you a hand is to be *silent* for ONE COUNT.

In two steps you can make a **QUARTER-REST**.

STEP ONE

Trace the following dotted lines:

STEP TWO

Add flags at top and bottom:

Notice that the Quarter-Rest *crosses* the *third* line.

Now draw six **QUARTER-RESTS**:

1   2   3   4   5   6

Hot Cross Buns

Nursery Rhyme

Hot   cross   buns!   Hot   cross   buns!   One - a - pen - ny,   two - a - pen - ny,   Hot   cross   buns!

Be careful to play both keys exactly together.
These are called DOUBLE NOTES.

This is a **SHARP**: ♯

A **SHARP** *raises* a note to the *nearest* key to the right (either *black* or *white*).

Play every **F♯** on your Piano

To make a **SHARP** follow these directions:
Draw a line: From 1 to 2
From 3 to 4
From 5 to 6
From 7 to 8

Around The World

When I am grown, I'll go to sea.

Come sail a - round the world with me!

Trace the following **SHARP** signs and you will see that the *center box* of each SHARP is on a **LINE**:

Trace the following SHARP signs and you will see that the *center box* of each SHARP is on a **SPACE**:

Now trace a SHARP on each **LINE** and **SPACE**:

Ice Cream Mountain

High on a moun-tain of ice cream I see Kings made of gum-drops in

choc - o - late cas - tles, And 'round them are lic - o - rice birds in a tree!

The Key of G

This is a **KEY SIGNATURE:** The **SHARPS** after the clef signs *(THE KEY SIGNATURE)* tell you that every **F** in the piece is to be played **F-SHARP**.

Santa Claus Time

Since this piece begins and ends on **G**, and every **F** is *sharped*, we are playing in the **KEY of G**.

To help you learn this new key, a dotted circle has been placed around every **F-SHARP**.

San - ta Claus is com-ing soon And he will sing a jol - ly tune, And bring to girls and boys Bright and shin - y toys.

44543

The First Recital Piece

This piece is to be memorized. You may play it for your family and your friends.

It is important to know how to perform a piece or a group of pieces. Here are some suggestions:

1. Walk to the piano in a natural, easy manner.

2. Sit down and place your feet together on the floor in front of the pedals.

3. Place your hands on the keyboard in position for the first notes.

4. **WAIT!** Think about how *loud* or *soft* and how *fast* or how *slow* the piece is to be played.

5. Then start to play.

6. Hold the last notes for their full value and then slowly return your hands to your lap.

Springtime

Let the right hand sing.

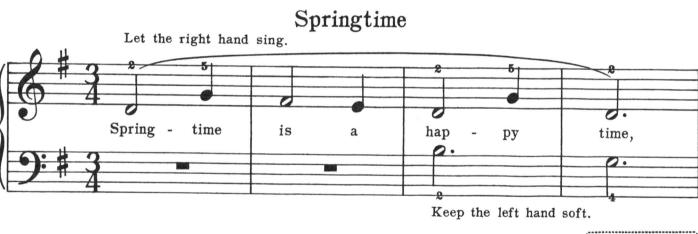

Spring - time   is   a   hap - py   time,

Keep the left hand soft.

Lift both hands for rests

Rob - ins   sing   on   the   wing.

All the flow - ers are so gay,

See the chil-dren at play.

This is a **TIE**. It is a curved line connecting two notes on the same line or space. It shows that only the first note is played. The second note is kept singing by being held for its full value without being sounded again.

Under the following notes write **P** for PLAY or **H** for HOLD:

My Prayer

Teach me to work, Teach me to play;

Teach me, O God, How to love and to pray.

The G Position

Here are new positions for **BOTH** hands.

Now we have { The RIGHT hand THUMB on the **G** *above* MIDDLE C.
The LEFT hand FIFTH FINGER on the **G** *below* MIDDLE C. }

When the hands are placed in this position it is called the **G POSITION**.

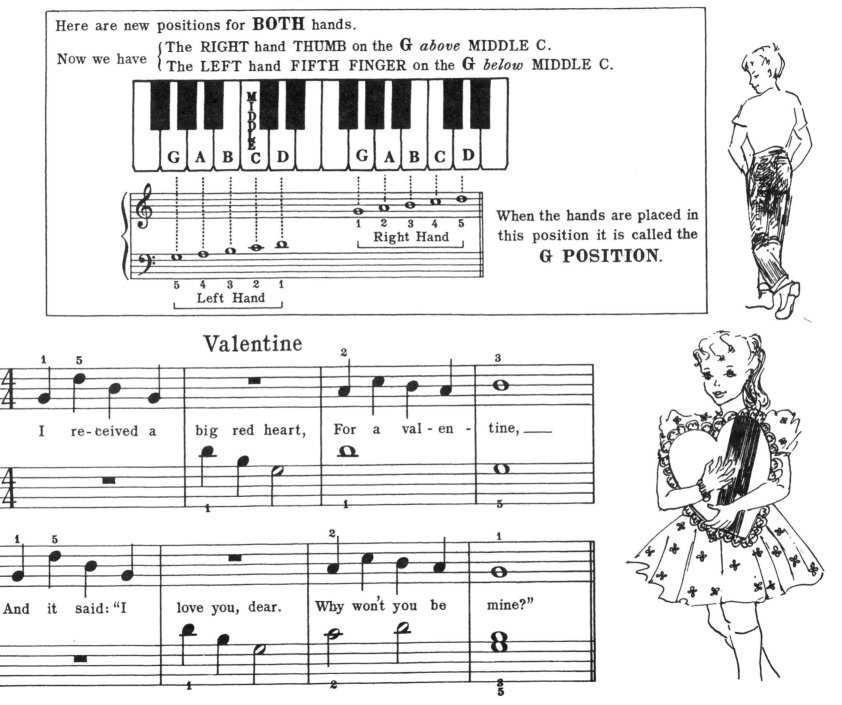

Valentine

I re-ceived a big red heart, For a val - en - tine, ____

And it said: "I love you, dear. Why won't you be mine?"

Halloween Pumpkin

The Flat Sign

A **FLAT** *lowers* a note to the *nearest* key to the left (either *black* or *white*).

This is a **FLAT**: ♭

Play every **B♭** on your Piano.

To make a **FLAT** follow these directions: Draw a line. From 1 to 2 and then From 3 through to 8.

Rocket Ship

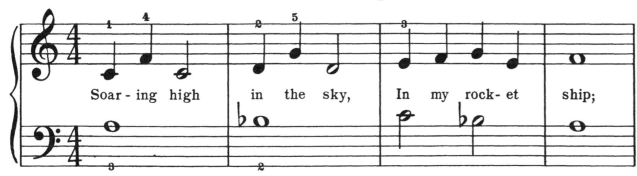

Soar-ing high | in the sky, | In my rock-et | ship;

See the moon! | See the stars! | What a thrill-ing | trip!

Trace the following **FLAT** signs and you will see that the *box* of each FLAT is on a **LINE**:

Trace the following FLAT signs and you will see that the *box* of each FLAT is on a **SPACE**:

Now trace a FLAT on each **LINE** and **SPACE**:

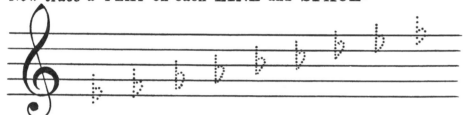

Mountain Climbing

I climbed a | moun-tain so | loft - y and | high,

That from the | top I could | reach to the | sky.

The Key of F

This is a
KEY SIGNATURE:

The **FLATS** after the clef signs (*THE KEY SIGNATURE*) tell you that every **B** in the piece is to be played **B-FLAT**.

Our Old Clock

Since this piece begins and ends on **F**, and every **B** is *flatted*, we are playing in the **KEY of F**.

To help you learn this new key, a dotted circle has been placed around every B-FLAT.

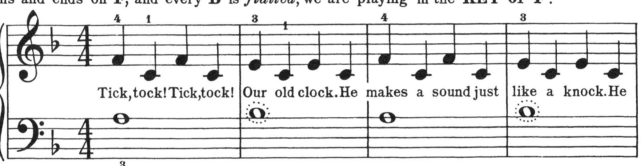

Tick, tock! Tick, tock! Our old clock. He makes a sound just like a knock. He stands so tall a - gainst the wall And says: Tick - tock!

The F Position

My Echo

8-------| is a sign that tells you to read the notes as they are written but to play them an octave higher. An octave is the distance between one key and the next key with the same letter name.

Peter, Peter, Pumpkin Eater

(Teach by rote)

Play the UP-STEM NOTES with the RIGHT HAND 3rd FINGER.
Play the DOWN-STEM NOTES with the LEFT HAND 3rd FINGER.

Nursery Rhyme

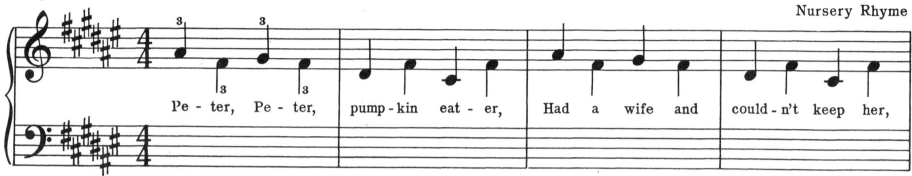

Pe - ter,   Pe - ter,   pump - kin eat - er,   Had   a   wife and   could - n't keep her,

Put her in a   pump - kin shell And   there he kept her   ver - y well!

Every note in this piece is played on a black key.

44543

The Natural Sign

This is a **NATURAL** sign: ♮

A **NATURAL** sign *changes* a note which has been sharped or flatted *back* to its original key name.

To make a **NATURAL** follow these directions:
Draw a line: From 1 to 2 to 3
From 4 to 5 to 6

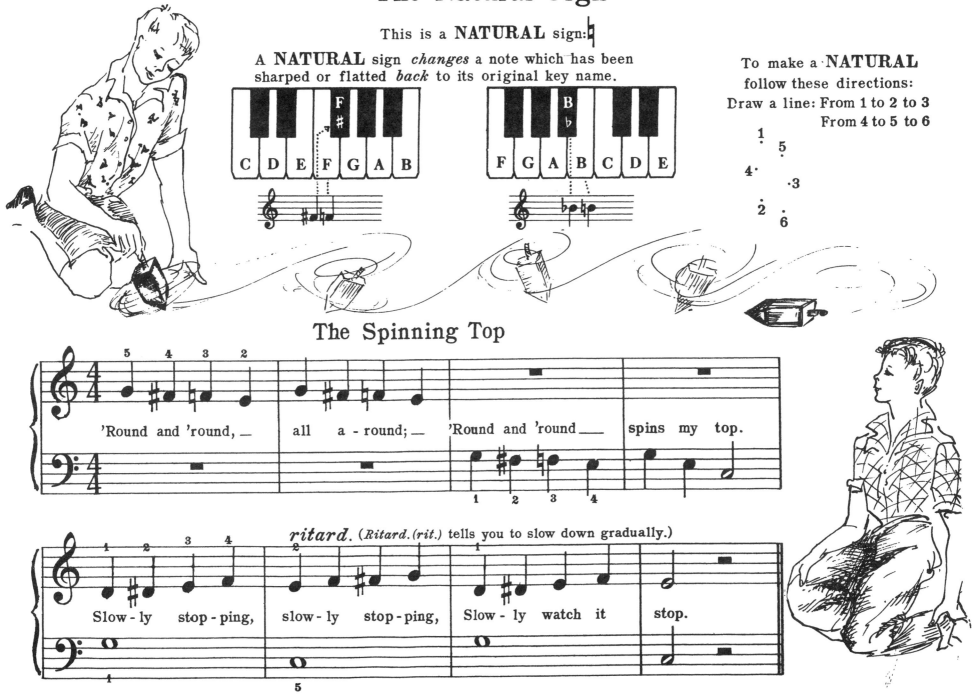

The Spinning Top

'Round and 'round, — all a - round; — 'Round and 'round ___ spins my top.

ritard. (*Ritard.* (*rit.*) tells you to slow down gradually.)

Slow - ly stop - ping, slow - ly stop - ping, Slow - ly watch it stop.

Trace the following **NATURAL** signs and you will see that the *center box* of each NATURAL is on a **LINE**:

Trace the following NATURAL signs and you will see that the *center box* of each NATURAL is on a **SPACE**:

Now trace a NATURAL on each **LINE** and **SPACE**:

Whoopee-ti-yi-yo!

Cowboy Song

1. As
I was a- ri- din' one morn- in' for pleas-ure, I
hat was throwed back and his spurs were a- jing- lin' And

see a cow punch- er a- ri- din' a- long. 2.His
as he ap- proached he was sing- in' a song.

1. *First ending* **2.** *Second ending*

long. 2.His

song.

*This is an incomplete measure. The missing beats will be found in the last measure.

44543

This is a **REPEAT** sign. The measures between the dots are played twice.

Sneaky Spook

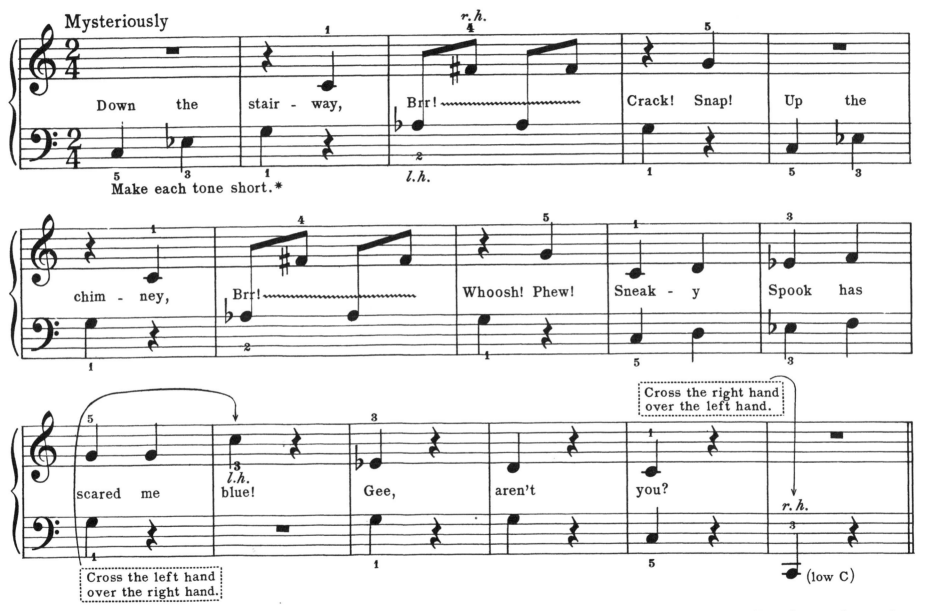

Mysteriously

Down the stair - way, Brr! Crack! Snap! Up the

Make each tone short.*

chim - ney, Brr! Whoosh! Phew! Sneak - y Spook has

scared me blue! Gee, aren't you?

Cross the right hand over the left hand.

Cross the left hand over the right hand.

(low C)

* This touch is called *staccato*. Lift your finger from each key quickly, as though the key were hot. This will produce a short, crisp *staccato* and will help make this piece sound mysterious.

CERTIFICATE AWARD

This Award certifies that

....

has successfully completed

"TEACH ME TO PLAY"

and is now ready to advance to

BOOK ONE

of

THE *Howard Kasschau Piano Course*

Teacher

*Date*_____